Duncan Aldred trained as an executive coach with Meyler Campbell and works as a coach, based mainly in London.

In his life before coaching, Duncan was a commercial lawyer specialising in fraud and finance-related disputes. He enjoyed the strategy, teamwork and urgency of litigating under pressure and was privileged to see different working styles up close, from Ferrari's F1 team to banking's Fred Goodwin and many others in between.

For over 30 years, Duncan was a partner in a City law firm in London and, for part of that time, he held a management role. He first had his own coach over 20 years ago and was struck then by the unique benefits coaching could bring.

Duncan's website is at www.duncanaldred.com.

To Mary A, Roger T, James B-H and Ann O, who took the trouble to try to teach me.

Duncan Aldred

IF YOU ONLY HAD TIME

What You'd Learn from an Executive Coach

AUSTIN MACAULEY PUBLISHERS™

LONDON • CAMBRIDGE • NEW YORK • SHARJAH

A CIP catalogue record for this title is available from the British Library.

ISBN 9781528979856 (Paperback)
ISBN 9781398406742 (Hardback)
ISBN 9781398406759 (ePub e-book)

www.austinmacauley.com

First Published (2021)
Austin Macauley Publishers Ltd
25 Canada Square
Canary Wharf
London
E14 5LQ

Work doesn't have to mean drudgery and stress. I'm indebted to those wonderful colleagues and clients who showed me this was possible, holding their heads above the fray and keeping a sense of humour. Thank you, too, to my coaching friends, Ann (surely, there's no better coach), Claudia, Emilio and Simon (they must come joint second). Simon has encouraged me more than he'd know. And thank you to Anne (with an e) who made my website possible and helped me to set up in the business of coaching.

Table of Contents

Spending time and money with the right executive coach could be the best investment you'd ever make. Here's what you'd be likely to learn.

Introduction
The Purpose of This Book

My mission is to help you recognise and rise to the challenges that come with working and progressing in an organisation.

To enjoy success in your career, you'll need a level of technical knowledge and skill and a degree of aptitude. Without those ingredients, you'll struggle to get the job done or to see it through. But unless you've chosen an unusual solo path, you'll need a further, vital ingredient.

This isn't about what you produce for your boss or your client, it's about how you pilot yourself through your career, pick your way through the challenges that come your way, and squeeze the most out of the chances you get to learn and develop.

This book shares with you what you'd be likely to hear if you had an executive coach on hand to help guide you through a number of typical challenges. Spending time (and money) with the right coach could be the wisest investment you'd ever make, but let's imagine that doesn't fit into your programme just now.

How the Book Works

In **Part 1**, I describe how a typical executive coach goes about the job of coaching.

Part 2 is about the groundwork you need to do to make an honest, objective assessment of yourself. If you were learning to play chess, you'd start by finding out what each piece could and couldn't do. Your task in getting to understand yourself is along the same lines, but with one very big difference. The subject you're studying is massively more interesting: your abilities aren't set in stone. You can learn, adapt, change and develop, so long as you take control and decide that's what you're going to do.

In **Part 3**, I run through twelve challenges you're most likely to face as you progress through your career. I've selected these from my experience as a coach and from my years of managing and team working in a law firm in London.

At the end of Part 2, and following each of the topics in Part 3, I suggest *Practical Steps*, points for action, which might emerge from a typical coaching programme.

Throughout the book, I'll mention other books you might read if you have the time.

Part 4 describes techniques you might use for tackling challenges, whether that's a challenge from my list of twelve or something else. Different devices work for different people and different questions, and different approaches will work for you, yourself, from time to time, depending on your mood.

I'm a strong believer in coaching and I have written this book to pass on some of the benefits that would come from working with a coach, if you had the opportunity to do that.

But no book could hope to give you all that time with the right coach might bring.

Part 1: What Is Coaching?

This book doesn't set out what a coach would *tell* you. A good coach would rarely *tell* you anything, as I'll explain below.

Coaching is not the same as mentoring.

When Odysseus went to fight in the Trojan War, he appointed Mentor as teacher and overseer to his son, Telemachus. That arrangement worked well, apparently. Mentor had far greater experience than the young Telemachus, and Mentor used that experience to positive effect; schooling and instructing the young boy.

Coaching doesn't work like that. The coach doesn't give instruction, the coach opens up ways of thinking.

That's not a cop-out. If you think about it, it makes sense. Mentor had such knowledge and wisdom that if he could impart just a fraction of what he knew to young Telemachus, the boy stood to be well prepared for life. You might think it follows that if you could just find your own Mentor, someone with detailed knowledge of the kind of work you do, you would hit the bull's eye. But pause for a few seconds and you'll see that that approach would miss a couple of important points. If all your mentor was capable of doing was to tell you how they'd done things when they did a job like yours, you'd see the limits to that kind of help straightaway. Is that knowledge up to date, or do you face new and different challenges?

And you'd miss out on a bit of sneaky psychology, too.

It's well established that, unless we're young children or we're in the army, we're much more likely to do things that we ourselves have suggested than we are to get on and do what someone else tells us we should do. If I told you smoking is bad for your health and you should give it up, the chances of you following that advice would be about zero. When you wake up one day and resolve for yourself that you're going to kick the habit, that's when you might get somewhere.

A decent coach will coax your thinking out of you with a 'non-directive' approach. If your coach uses language like 'What you should do is…', they're going way off track. If they've got a conscience, they'll have alarm bells ringing in their mind, warning them to stop *telling* and start *asking*.

The coach knows they need to respond to warnings like that straightaway. It's simply not possible to coach properly with a mind that's buzzing with any other 'noise'.

Coaches are trained to clear their minds so that all their thinking is focused on the client, and to 'Listen' (with a capital 'L'). There are two aspects to that. Before a coaching session, the coach will try to empty their mind of current clutter that's not relevant for you; and, through the session, they'll be avoiding the 'Ping-Pong' of normal conversation. That second point is about the 'queuing to talk' that we all do in usual conversation, not taking in the whole of what someone else is saying, but timing when we're going to cut in to respond. And somewhere in the same family is the Park Run question, asked only because the questioner has their own story to tell. "Have you been on one of these Park Runs?"'

"No?"

"I went on one yesterday…I find my times improve every week…"

You shouldn't get any of that 'Let me tell you about me!' from a coach. Far from promoting themselves, they'll be focusing on you and where you want to get to. They might take part in lots of Park Runs, but you're unlikely to find out unless the coach thinks it would somehow be useful to you to know about it.

You can see from this that a coach offers you something different from a chat. Your coach will be listening to you more carefully than most other people in your life ever do, and their focus will be on you. The pace of the dialogue will be slower than you're used to in a business meeting or a social conversation. And if the coach is doing their job properly, you'll feel free to say what comes to mind, confident you're not going to be judged and confident the coach won't share what you talk about with anyone else.

The slower pace is important. In the rest of our lives, we spend most of our time in a hurry. Maybe a lot of the stuff we get on with day-to-day can be done without much thought, but your coach isn't operating in that superficial First Brain territory that Daniel Kahneman wrote about in, *Thinking, Fast and Slow* (Penguin Books, 2012) where motorway driving is so easy the car seems to drive itself. Your coach is encouraging you to engage your 'Second Brain' and do some real thinking. That can't be done in a rush.

Can you imagine a conversation where, hand on heart, you don't make any judgement in your own mind about the person who's talking to you or about what they're telling you? For a

19

coach, that kind of judging would count as irrelevant 'noise' that's going to get in the way, so their training is to avoid it.

And all this happens behind a screen of confidentiality. You're free to tell anyone about what you discuss in your coaching sessions, but to benefit from coaching, you need to be able to speak freely and you can't sensibly do that unless you trust your coach to keep what you discuss private between you.

A coach is on your side, but coaching is not about being nice. It can be at its most valuable when it challenges you. When a coach listens to you and then 'asks for your permission', with polite words such as "Can I question what you've just said?", you're on notice that you're going to hear something very direct, and, if you deal with it in the right way, potentially of great use to you.

Having started with what's *not* coaching, a quick word about what a coach can't do. Your executive coach is not a medical adviser; and a coach won't be able to help you achieve anything useful unless you're prepared to engage with the process and contribute fully to it. But if you make that positive choice with a coach who's right for you, you have lots to gain.

Part 2: Before You Start, Understand Yourself

Before you dive into identifying what you want to change, and how you want things to be, you have some preliminary work to do.

Who are you? What are you like? And what situation do you find yourself in?

This bit's important. As you set out on your mission to achieve your potential, it's vital to have an understanding of what materials you'll be working with.

On page twenty-eight, I suggest *Practical Steps* to help you understand yourself.

2.1: Personality Profiling (or Not!)

Are you naturally an extrovert or an introvert? A leader or a follower? A creator of ideas or an implementer of the ideas of others? The categories of personality types go on. If you have the opportunity to explore your own profile with one of the many tests that are available, the chances are you won't be shocked by the results. Much more likely, the results will confirm what you already thought, or they'll ring bells.

The most respected tool for assessing how you're likely to behave in different situations is the *Myers-Briggs Type Indicator Instrument (MBTI)* (https://www.myersbriggs.org). The MBTI tool was first developed by Isabel Briggs Myers in the 1940s, building on Carl Jung's (1920s) theory of psychological type. The Indicator was initially published in 1962, and millions of people around the world have made use of it since then.

To produce a useful result, the Myers-Briggs test has to be administered by someone with specific training, who is able to make a proper assessment of the answers to a long list of carefully crafted multiple choice questions.

Whatever verdict emerges from any test you take, don't waste time and energy making judgements about yourself. Being one personality type rather than another doesn't make you a better or worse person; it simply makes you more of a natural for some situations than others.

It's important, anyway, that you see those tests for what they are. They're a snapshot in time and, generally, the only person who's contributed a view is you yourself, so they might not be objective.

If you memorise your profile and wear that as a badge for the rest of your life, you're missing the point. At best, personality profiling helps you find your default inclinations. For example, you might learn that, left to your own devices, you'd be more comfortable sitting on your sofa at home than giving a presentation to a room full of people. As is so often the case, this information has no value by itself, it's what you do with it that counts. If you decide to give yourself a nudge to get off the sofa, and maybe get training or guidance on how best to deliver a speech, then that's when you're getting somewhere. Once you've followed through on that decision, you'll improve your skills, which will build your confidence and reduce your inclination to avoid public speaking. You'll also have demonstrated to yourself that you have the ability to develop, that you're not condemned to carry the same baggage forever.

Instead of navigating your way through personality tests, trying hard to spot the patterns so you can emerge with the most enviable profile for your particular world, I recommend you do something else. Take a few quiet minutes to think for yourself about the different situations you find yourself in. When are you at your most comfortable? When do you start to feel under pressure? And when do you see 'red mist'? When are you bored, and when are you so wrapped up in what you're doing that you don't notice time going by? When do you feel you've achieved something worthwhile?

As well as listening to yourself, listen and watch for the signals others give you about the impact you're having on them. Most of the time, those signals won't be fully articulated, but they'll be clues for you to read, if you care to do that. Don't block out what people say about you, it might be information you can put to very good use.

2.2: An Honest CV

Objectively, what have you achieved, and what situation are you in? What are your skills, and what are you less good at? When you think this through, don't be shy about trumpeting what you're proud of, and don't be easy on yourself when you're assessing your weaknesses: there's little value in all this if you're not honest.

I recommend you write down this CV using separate headings to list characteristics and achievements you're proud of and others that you see as less positive. Get everything out on the table. Just like with a coach, you're safe – if you want to, you can make your lists and thoughts confidential, and share them with no one else.

I dare you to go further with this 'private' CV. What do you 'need'? One obvious candidate for that list might be 'money'. If it is – how much? But what else do you need to make you happy? What matters to you? Think of situations where you have felt 'in your element'. Were you with others, or were you operating quietly, alone?

When have you felt less comfortable, and what was it that made you feel that way?

A typical CV will list exam results and, while it's rare to see an IQ test score, the purpose is usually to show how good you are at passing exams or how 'intelligent' you are. Daniel Goleman is an academic and writer who has gathered together a great deal of thinking on 'emotional intelligence', starting with his first book on the topic, *Emotional Intelligence* (Bantam Books, 1995). Under that heading of emotional intelligence, Goleman included self-awareness, self-control and empathy, and the arts of listening, resolving conflicts and cooperation.

Things have moved on in this area since 1995. Rather than reading Goleman's original book, you'll find much more readable introductions to the principles at the heart of emotional intelligence online, for example on the Harvard Business School website.

The thinking goes that, for any given occupation, there's a limit to how much IQ-type 'intelligence' is useful and, beyond that limit, what really makes a person any better at that activity is greater *emotional* intelligence. For a commercial lawyer, for example, there is huge value in an ability to listen to and understand a client, an ability to work in a team and an ability to read other people – not things reflected in an IQ test or taught at law school.

Don't leave out emotional intelligence when you're compiling your CV for yourself. And don't despair if, being honest with yourself, you identify an area where you might not be a resounding success. Give yourself a pat on the back for making the discovery and set about finding a way to make things better.

One of the benefits of considering what you're good and bad at and where your enthusiasms lie is it can help you appreciate that there are other people just like you and there are other people who are different from you. That doesn't make any particular type right or wrong, but just differently equipped for any given challenge.

Understand Yourself: Practical Steps

1. Set up a document that you'll find easy to access, to add to and to change
2. Ask yourself:
   - *What am I good at?*
   - *What am I not so good at?*
   - *What parts of my job do I look forward to/ enjoy?*
   - *What parts of my job do I dread?*
   - *What do other people say about me?*
3. Look at the evidence you've gathered
4. Imagine it's not about you but a character in a novel
5. How would you describe this person as you set out to guide them?

Part 3: The Typical Coaching Challenges

In this section, I set out a number of challenges that are the everyday business of an executive coach. You might call them *problems* but the first thing a coach would do would be to get you to frame things in a positive way. I suggest ways of meeting these challenges with 'Practical Steps' at the end of each topic.

3.1: Set Your Goal

This challenge is first on the list for two reasons. Many of us find it the most difficult; and, once you have your answer, that answer provides the purpose for everything else you do, like drawing thread through a needle.

Stephen R Covey wrote the entertaining book: *The 7 Habits of Highly Effective People* (Simon & Schuster, 1989). In his section on 'Begin with the End in Mind', he invites us to imagine we're sitting at our own funeral and asks us what we'd like to hear said about ourselves.

I'll put the same question less dramatically.

How do you want to 'feel' about your career and the way you've spent your time? Set a date somewhere in the future…maybe in three years, five years, or on the day you retire. Imagine you're looking back from that date. What will make you feel you've spent your time well? What will frustrate you?

Now's the time to set your sights and steer a course that will be in tune with those thoughts.

You can be as high-flown as you like when you start your thinking on this topic. Maybe there's a particular charity you'd like to support. It could be you conclude that you'd like to spend every waking hour working for that charity, starting now. More likely, you might build around what that charity stands for, designing a future that is smoothly in line with those values, like the grain in a piece of wood, and that might give you a platform to promote those values.

Imagine yourself in a shoe shop, trying on shoes for size and style. How would you feel walking home in this pair? Are they really 'you'? From deciding what you 'don't' want, and pressing yourself to explain why, you're getting closer to deciding what you'll be aiming for.

You might have a single guiding light that will draw you forward or, more likely, you'll have more than one thing on a list that defines your 'Goal'. Check that the different elements aren't in conflict with each other or be prepared to revise them so that they're in tune.

Decide now, on a programme for checking in with yourself, to assess whether you're on course for achieving your Goal, whether you need to make changes to get back on track, and whether the Goal needs to be altered. You'll need to ask yourself 'If I'm heading in the right direction, how should things look in three, six or twelve months' time?' You might think of your overall Goal as your Goal with a capital 'G', and the points along the way as your shorter term 'goals'.

You can set your own milestones, and they can be hugely valuable to keep you honest and to give you encouragement.

Your Goal, once set, won't achieve itself. It may be that you don't share your thinking with anyone else. Whether you share that thinking or keep it to yourself, it'll be up to you whether you truly set about achieving your Goal.

Set Your Goal: Practical Steps

Ask yourself:

- *How do I want to feel about my career five years from now?*
- *On the day I retire, how do I want to feel about the way I've spent my working life?*
- *What am I likely to regret, if I change nothing?*
- *What will I have to change to make my Goal a realistic Goal?*
- *How will I know I'm on the right track for achieving my Goal? What will I have changed and what will my world look like? When?*

3.2: Change

Are you dissatisfied enough to change?

Whatever it is you want to change, and whether that change will involve just you alone or others, it's vital to respect the power of inertia.

There's the story about the child who's reached the age of 7 and still hasn't spoken a word. Then, out of the blue, one mealtime, he announces to his family, "This soup is cold!" His shocked and confused parents want an explanation for those years of silence. "Why haven't you spoken in all this time?" The son calmly replies, "Everything was all right until now."

At Harvard Business School, they talk about the size of the 'D'. In this context, D stands for Dissatisfaction. The thinking goes that, the greater the size of the 'D' (dissatisfaction with the status quo), the more likely we are to accept the need for change and the more likely that change will actually be seen through. If the soup hadn't been cold, the boy might still be keeping his powder dry, not seeing any advantage in taking the trouble to break his silence. It will help to have a clear belief that things will be better following the change, than without it. More than that, you need to think things will be so much better that the effort and disruption of making the change will be worth your while.

Be honest with yourself

David Maister (*Strategy and the Fat Smoker* – Spangle Press, 2008) was one of the most prominent business thinkers in the early years of the 21st Century. Maister brought a refreshing voice to the subject of change with his 'Fat Smoker' presentation, in which he declared that he stood before his audience as a man who knew that he'd be healthier if he lost weight and gave up smoking, but he'd decided to do neither of those things. He was clear that he was making his own choices and that he accepted responsibility for making them.

What Maister highlighted was that if individuals and businesses were drifting aimlessly and failing to make positive changes, they were, by default, making a choice. He urged them to open their eyes to the choices they were making and to take responsibility for those choices. Maister also stressed the distinction between, on the one hand, deciding intellectually that change would be a good idea and, on the other hand, actually taking the action needed to bring about that change.

Challenge yourself – *and be honest* – about whatever it is you think you'd like to change. Maybe, given a magic wand, you'd lose weight, or perhaps it's becoming wearing to start every meeting with an apology for being late and you'd like to be one of those people who are ready and there on time. If the days go by and that waistband's still just as tight, or you're still just that couple of minutes late attending your meetings, open your eyes to the fact that whatever fine thoughts you're juggling in your mind, the reality is, you're making a choice *not* to change.

Change: Practical Steps

Ask yourself:

- *How will I know when I've achieved this change (What will things look like/feel like)?*
- *In what ways will things look/feel better than they do now?*
- *What will I need to do differently to achieve this change?*
- *Am I really prepared to do what's needed?*

If your honest answer to the final question is 'No', stop wasting your time on wishful thinking, admit to yourself that you're not willing to pay the price for that change that would be nice-to-have, and get on with something else instead.

3.3: Step Up

Congratulations! You were so good at what you were doing before; you've been promoted to do something quite different.

Let go of your comfort blanket

Typically, you'll have done well enough to be noticed in your previous role, and felt comfortable, because you've been on top of the detail. Moving up in an organisation usually means getting less time to know the detail. It's more about the bigger picture, exercising judgement, and delegating.

You can feel naked now, without all those details to immerse yourself in. There was a comfort that came from all that research and background reading. Even a sense of justice: it was only right that you felt confident of your subject after you'd put in all those hours on the detail.

Stand back and assess what your new role calls for. The chances are it won't be 'the same as before plus...' It's likely you'll need to say goodbye to that familiar, comforting work on the minutiae; step up and operate in a different way. As you get on with tackling this change, give yourself credit for leaving your comfort zone. We like to do what we already do well, but you've got a choice to make, stick with what you know you're good at, or accept the challenge to learn, develop and advance your career.

If you need more of a nudge to change, ask yourself what you're now being *paid* to do. Will the firm really be happy for you to carry on just as before? Or is it looking for something different from you now?

Step up...to what?

Unskilled jobs often come with a highly prescriptive regime. You're drilled on exactly what to do at your point on the conveyor belt. You know what success (and failure) will look like.

The further you move up the scale, the greater the uncertainty about what's expected of you.

In this territory where the charts aren't so clear, it makes sense to use whatever guidance is available. Who (apart from you) will decide whether you've done the job well? What are they expecting from you, and how will they gauge your success? Can you ask them?

The more your career progresses, the more space – and call – there'll be for you to come up with ideas yourself. Whether it's your stakeholders or you who come up with the definition of your role, it will be healthy to share a common understanding about it.

Up, and beyond

In a dynamic world, you and your firm need to keep moving, or risk being left behind. What more can you achieve from this new platform you've been given? What else do you think you could usefully do, over and above the role that's been set out for you?

To learn what might be possible, you'll need to look beyond your firm, to find out what's going on out there and what people are thinking and planning for the future. What should you be reading? Who should you be talking – and listening – to?

Keep your momentum, keep the initiative, keep challenging yourself, and keep learning. What will be next after this?

Step up: practical steps

1. Let go of your comfort blanket
2. Ask yourself:
   - *What does my boss expect of me in this new role?*
   - *What can I do* beyond *that?*
   - *Where are my sources of learning?*
   - *Where's my network?*
   - *After this?*

3.4: Control Your Inner Voice

Have you got a doubting voice in your head, an 'inner voice', that's your very own pundit, sagely telling you in advance just what can go wrong and what a mess you're going to make of things?

Maybe you're about to start a presentation when that unseen companion grabs your attention. What if you dry up? What if you can't think of anything to say apart from the words that appear on your slides? What if you suddenly can't even read those words you've already written?

In that mood, this inner voice hijacks your thoughts, cranks up the 'red mist' and steals from you your power to think clearly.

You might recognise the same companion from other areas of your life. Your doubting voice might haunt your attempts at baking ('However hard I try, I'm never going to make decent pastry'); and if you play sport, the chances are this inner voice is a familiar partner ('I know what I'm like. I'm going to make a mess of this shot. The ball's going to go a couple of metres, or it'll go sailing over the green. One thing's for sure, it won't end up anywhere near the hole!').

It was in the world of sport that W. Timothy Gallwey started to explore this topic. His book *The Inner Game of*

Tennis (Pan Books, 1986) rang bells with lots of people, and it was easy to see the links from tennis to other sports and then to other areas of life, including business. Steve Peters' *The Chimp Paradox* (Random House, 2011) provides a more readable and entertaining exploration of this topic.

It's within your power to turn your doubting inner voice around, and to convert it into a strong and useful ally. Don't wait, though, until you're starting that presentation, before you decide to take control.

We've all got one

As with many challenges, it can be helpful to appreciate that we all have this inner voice. At its most basic level, it can help by telling us that something we're about to do is dangerous. It's embarrassing to admit it, but the human brain hasn't evolved as quickly as some aspects of the world around us, and the warning system that might have saved our lives 200,000 years ago isn't as sophisticated as we'd like it to be if we could re-design and update it today.

Respect it for what it is

One response to the negative inner voice would be to try to shut it out. Tell it that it hasn't got a ticket and can't come in. Stick your fingers in your ears and say 'LaLaLa!' But you can do much better than that.

The starting point is to respect why the voice exists and why it has decided to make itself heard at this particular time. And then you need to accept that the system's a bit out of date and you have to forgive it for conveying its message in a way that, to your mind, is hugely ham-fisted.

If you're about to give your presentation, it might be quite logical to think 'This is a sophisticated audience that will see straight through me if I fail to show mastery of my subject, so I need to get this right!'. But all the inner-voice warning system will do will be to sound alarm bells and flash red warning lights to tell you there's danger. If you don't find a way of working with your inner voice, those alarm bells and red lights will become louder and brighter and get in the way of what you really need to do to produce your best performance.

Acknowledge and challenge it, and make the timing your own

From reflecting on who you are and what you're like [see Part 2 of this book], you'll have an idea of when your inner voice is likely to make an appearance. Apart from the negative nature of its message when it comes on the scene, there's the fact that you have no control over whether or when it will turn up and there's the apprehension that, if it does decide to arrive, it might swamp your thoughts.

To pluck some timing from the air, three weeks before your presentation, mentally step back from the challenge you've taken on. Apart from thinking about what you'll have to say, consider how you're feeling about the event. Invite your inner voice to this preparation session.

Now is the time to have that thought about the need to show you're the master of your subject. Challenge your inner voice with questions. 'You're saying it could go wrong. What things are you talking about?' Press yourself for answers, and take control. Consider, in turn, each 'fear' you come up with, and mentally either add it to a list headed 'Things I can prepare for' or drop it into a bin for 'Things I can't control (so there's no point worrying about)'.

Then go to work on the preparations.

If you dictate the timing in this way, and if you make your brain do more than just issue a warning that there's something to worry about, you're getting the best out of your inner voice and upgrading it for use in the 21st Century. If you then buckle down to the preparation, you'll give your inner voice less cause to turn up out of the blue, and you'll have a clear and logical answer to put it in its place if it does.

Control your inner voice: practical steps

1. Listen to yourself; get to know your 'inner voice'.
2. In what kinds of situations does it tend to appear?
3. How does it make you feel?
4. Is it useful to you?
5. Don't let your inner voice lie in wait and ambush you, make it engage with you at a time of your choosing.
6. Respect the warning signs; take the trouble to interpret what they mean.
7. Act on the warnings. The alarm bell will stop ringing when it has achieved its purpose.
8. Make friends with your inner voice. Don't tolerate it as a bully; make it a sparring partner you call upon to keep yourself sharp.

3.5: Get Serious

People are sometimes embarrassed to raise this topic. After all, you're thinking, 'it's *only* me!' The question can be put as 'How do I do *Gravitas*?' This often comes to mind because you've been promoted to a more senior role (see **Step Up** at **3.3**).

Gravitas isn't about bossing people around. It's about being taken seriously and being listened to.

In his book *Principles* (Simon & Schuster, 2017), Ray Dalio talks about colleagues who are 'believable'. He doesn't mean they're the ones who tell the truth (as opposed to the others who don't). He's referring to individuals who clearly have the knowledge and expertise to make their thoughts and opinions valuable.

Ask yourself whether you really know what you're talking about. Are you worth listening to, and not just faking it? Positive answers to these questions mean you've convinced the most important person – yourself. The rest is easy. Armed with the knowledge that you *deserve* to be taken seriously, it's down to practicalities. Do it your own way – be true to your own personality, don't try to copy anyone else.

Get serious: practical steps

1. Use fewer words, not more
2. Speak clearly, not loudly
3. Don't rush
4. Listen first; don't be afraid to speak last
5. Don't say 'It's only me!'

3.6: Manage Your Brand

For most people, a large part of business success comes through effective teamwork. Without the ability to work well with others, we are limited to producing whatever we can as solo operators.

It makes sense to combine your efforts with colleagues, but it's important, from time to time, to reflect on where you stand as an individual. There are a number of reasons why this is a good idea.

Imagine that, suddenly, five years have gone by and you're looking back at how your career has developed (or not). Won't you want to feel that it hasn't all just happened by accident, but that you've stopped from time to time to examine your situation, to check in with yourself on where you're trying to get to, and settle on what you're going to do to get yourself there?

This selfish thinking needs to be handled carefully. You don't want to overdo it and take your focus permanently away from the benefits and enjoyment of working with colleagues. But no one else is going to manage your career for you, so if anyone's going to do this assessment and planning, it'll have to be you.

Your team can provide you with support and reassurance, but it can also harbour a hidden danger. Every time you use 'We' and 'Our' to describe your efforts and ambitions, you're building the group, but what about 'you'? Are you using your colleagues as a shield and hiding behind some idea of joint responsibility? Are you shying away from accountability for what you've done and not done yourself?

Be honest with yourself.

Having put yourself on the spot, how about doing yourself justice? From time to time, it might be fair to acknowledge (whether it's just to yourself or to others, too) your own role in what's been achieved and what's planned. You'll have to judge the communications, but how can you expect anyone to reach positive conclusions about you if they've no idea about what you've done?

'I' and 'Me' can be the right words to use, to take responsibility (even where that's for something good).

Manage your brand: practical steps

1. Ask yourself:
    - *How do I want colleagues and clients to see me?*
    - *How do they see me now?*
    - *What is my Goal for my career?*
    - *Who will make career decisions about me?*
    - *How can I get my good stuff noticed?*
2. Sometimes, 'I', not 'We'

3.7: Lead

What kind of people will you be leading? What kind of leadership will benefit them and your firm?

Will Carling captained the England rugby team, 59 times between 1988 and 1996, with a high level of success. In a question-and-answer session, he was asked what words he could possibly find, as the leader of his national side, to inspire his troops as they headed out onto the field of battle. His answer was considered, and it wasn't what anyone in the room expected. Carling explained that, at that level of his sport, everyone on the pitch was a leader. Each player knew what he had to do. The leader's role was to maintain tone and cohesiveness. It wasn't to shout at anyone.

Jean Todt is a thoughtful man in a (literally) fast-moving world. He was appointed to the highest rank of France's Legion d'Honneur following the first two chapters of his career in motorsport, in which he was a successful rally co-driver, developing the iconic Peugeot 205 and then created and led a Peugeot team, which for many years, dominated the Le Mans 24 hours endurance event. Post-Peugeot, Jean led the Ferrari F1 team to huge success when Formula One was at its most exciting.

To be in a meeting with Jean at Ferrari was a privilege. He surrounded himself with experts. He respected those experts; he created calm; he asked questions, and he drew the very best from each person around the table.

Contrast Carling and Todt with the brand of leader we see most on TV – the chef in charge of a kitchen. Typically, they transmit, they don't receive. Asked why it made sense to harangue a teenager on his staff, Marcus Wareing (a very pleasant man whose teams create sublime food) explained that the lad just needed telling, it was the only way he'd learn. Of the two of them, Wareing had the monopoly in skill and experience.

And then there was Fred Goodwin. You didn't get stronger than Fred. But what a mess he made. We all agree now, but not so many people said anything at the time. It wasn't that nobody noticed – he was much disliked and dubbed 'Fred the Shred' long before he joined The Royal Bank of Scotland – but his style of leadership put up with no questioning. While Fred's strong style took his bank in a definite direction (and temporarily earned him a knighthood), it flatly discouraged contributions from others and robbed the bank of what they would have had to give.

What kind of leadership does your firm need?

Do the people you're leading just need to be taught, or instructed what to do, or could they be making a positive contribution to the firm if only you encouraged them to do that?

Do you frighten people, or do you create an atmosphere of calm and trust in which colleagues dare to put ideas forward even when they might not be perfect?

When did someone working for you last tell you that you might be wrong?

My friend and fellow-coach Emilio Galli-Zugaro has written interestingly about leadership and about how the so-called leader who sees their job as 'telling' is missing the point. Cleverly, Emilio enlists the help of one of his daughters to underline his message, from the next generation's point of view (Emilio Galli-Zugaro, Clementina Galli-Zugaro – *The Listening Leader*, FT Publishing, 2017).

Don't forget

Think about bosses you've worked for in the past. What frustrated you about them? What impressed you? What did they do that made it easier for you to do your job?

It's a people thing

Warning: managing people takes time. And it involves people.

Do you really see yourself having the skills and the patience to listen properly to your team, to properly understand each of the individuals who report to you, and to get to the point where they will turn to you for help when they need it?

Sometimes you can take shortcuts. Briefing the whole team at one go will mean you say things once and they've all got the message. But are the channels of communication really open?

To properly lead, you need to have a good feeling for those following you and what shape they're in. If keeping track takes you away from your own desk and you resent that, maybe you're not cut out to be a leader, after all. To be a leader in more than just name, you will need to invest time to speak to your reports, and to listen to them, in a place where they feel they can speak safely, and tell you their concerns, if they have any.

This isn't just about being kind to people, it makes financial sense. It is far better to have early warning of difficulties in the team than to hear nothing until there's a resignation.

Get to know your team. Stay in touch with them. And a challenge: if you have it in you to ask the question 'What can I do to help you?' you'll really be getting somewhere.

A confident boss will dare to open the door to thoughts and ideas from their reports and reap all the benefits from that.

While you're looking at your colleagues, they'll be looking at you. Do you have a smile on your face, or do you have all the cares of the world on your shoulders? You can change their mood without saying a word: who wants to work for a boss who looks downcast and defeated? As a leader, you're never off stage.

The skill of the middle-leader

Whatever your leadership role, the chances are, you're not in absolute control but have someone else to answer to.

What's the point of your role? Is it just to pass on to your troops the very same message that's been handed down to you? Surely, an email could do that job. Your challenge will be to find how to get the best out of your team. That won't come from parroting what your boss has told you. You need to know your team and how best to communicate with them.

Back your own judgement. You might decide the word from above has to be translated into something that will work for your colleagues…or maybe, you know it won't help to pass that particular message on at all.

Leading can be lonely

Typically, promotion to a leadership role separates you from colleagues who have been your peers and friends. The change in those relationships can make a very big difference to your world.

If an old friend asks the new you whether you've got time for lunch or a chat, there's a chance now that they'll want to take some time with you in your role as the boss.

You might be looking for an hour off from the burden of being the leader, to let off steam and speak your mind without restriction, but being the leader reduces your options. If you think you can carry on as before and share all that you're thinking with those colleagues who now have you as their manager, you'll need to think again. You can't gossip one day and do performance reviews the next.

Being a leader can feel most lonely when you have difficult decisions to take affecting other people, perhaps about pay, promotions, redundancies or dismissals. It wouldn't be unusual for you to resent it when you find your job comes with an emotional burden that's new to you. Most likely, no one told you you'd find it very uncomfortable to break the news to a colleague that they're going to be out of work. You'll have found your job testing in different ways in the past, but this kind of discomfort might be new to you.

The self-effacing leader

Some leadership positions are hotly contested. Others are roles that have to be filled by someone, and that someone just happens to be you. You didn't push yourself forward, but as they've asked you to take on the job, you suppose you'll do it.

If this is you, you're a danger to all concerned; a wallflower leader. You'll occupy the place, take the pay, but not do any leading.

Get over yourself and get on with the job!

A leader leads

There are different styles of leadership but, whatever way you choose, you've got to take the responsibility and get on with it. Promotion to a leadership role is much more than a pay rise or a new label. You'll be on stage. Your moods will be noticed and remembered. Your way of dealing with people will be copied.

Colleagues will look to you for fairness and reassurance but, above all, they'll look to you to lead. To underline that message, ask yourself what you're now being *paid* to do.

If you don't want to lead, don't take the job.

Lead: practical steps

Ask yourself:

- *What kind of leadership is needed here?*
- *What can I learn from people who've led me?*
- *Do I have time and energy left over for my colleagues?*
- *Do I have capacity for empathy (and can I be bothered to tune-in to how my colleagues see things)?*
- *When did I ask 'What can I do to help?'*

- *What would my team say about me as their leader?*
- *Does my team know what we're aiming for?*
- *If there was a problem, would they tell me?*
- *What am I being* paid *to do?*

3.8: Delegate

It's something new

You probably got to where you are now by being a very successful solo operator.

Your academic exams weren't a team effort. School, university and college performance is largely assessed as a competition between individuals. Some institutions will give you a ranking. Even where that didn't happen, you'll have been used to discussing your results with your friends and working out a pecking order. It's been you against the world.

Those exam results were the core of your early CVs, the ones you put together when you were looking for work experience and for your first job. You knew you needed to show you'd done more than take exams, and you tried hard to tack on evidence of teamwork and leadership. But those extra items were the icing on the cake, the currency you needed to get to where you wanted to go was the exam stuff. Typically, you'd have done your reading and much of your learning alone and you'd have sat at a very small desk- for-one to write your answers.

Delegation is a new thing for most us when we get to our first job. We didn't see it in the classroom, and you could spend a lot of time in 'CV'-enhancing sports teams without coming across it.

In a junior role, as well as getting on with your job, you have the luxury of being an observer. What kinds of tasks do you see being delegated? What is said by the people doing the delegating and by the people who are taking on the tasks? Does it look efficient to you? Could you do better?

What behaviour do you see in between work on specific tasks? Do the senior people in your firm only notice the existence of the juniors when they want to shovel something off their own desk? Or do they acknowledge those junior people even on days when they don't need anything from them?

Being lazy can help!

To find delegating easy, it helps to be ever so slightly lazy. If you are driven to cover every last detail yourself, so that you know that it's right, you need to accept that you'll limit your output to what you yourself can produce.

Imagine a chef who insists on preparing and cooking all the ingredients for all the courses themselves, setting the cutlery neatly on the tables (because only they know how), taking orders, delivering food to the tables and greeting the customers at the door. What kind of restaurant could that be? I picture a frazzled chef in a very tiny restaurant that doesn't stay in business long. You can do better than that.

The chances are you got your current role because you convinced someone you were good at chopping carrots (or some office-based equivalent of that). The challenge for you now, is to step up from carrot-chopping and let the next person have a go. This means leaving behind something you've been good at, which can be uncomfortable. Without a determined effort, you can easily fall back into doing what's familiar and, whether you're conscious of it or not, the thought will be lurking somewhere that if you say goodbye to what you used to do, you'll be stepping out into unknown territory and cutting yourself off from any route back.

Is it really for you?

Be honest with yourself. Is delegating to other people really for you? It might be that you'd be happier staying where you are with your job and being responsible just for yourself. That can be a perfectly valid choice. But if that's the choice you make, make it with your eyes open, knowing that you'll be limiting what your job can offer you.

If you're serious about progressing in your career, seize this opportunity, and take up the challenge.

An opportunity to delegate is more than a means for getting the immediate task completed. It's a chance for you to develop an important skill and to develop a team. Think of it as though you're guiding your team through an obstacle course. Decide at the outset that you'll give yourself maximum points for arriving at the finishing tape, having successfully completed the task but – just as important – with a happy team that's gained from the experience.

Here's your chance to influence someone else's day in the office. You'll be able to make choices about how you do your delegating. How much will you share about what's really needed; the broader context and the timetable? It's for you to gauge what it will be worthwhile to share with the team. If you're lucky, and the calibre of your colleagues means you can properly involve them in the bigger picture, you stand to benefit in so many ways. You might get suggestions for how to get the job done more efficiently or to a better standard, you'll open up a channel of communication and you'll be building a stronger, better-experienced team for next time.

Don't forget

Your own experience of having tasks delegated to you is hugely valuable. Good and bad. Don't waste it!

What was the worst thing about being in a junior role and being given tasks to complete? Were you terrified that you weren't sure exactly what was needed, whether you had the skills or information necessary to get the job done? Did you ever stay late at your desk, anxious to finish the task before you dared to head for home, even though you didn't have any idea of the deadline? Did you ever have a time when you were fairly sure you'd heard the instructions correctly, but the only thing you were really certain about was that you couldn't risk the embarrassment of checking if you were on the right track?

Or you might have had a boss who took a couple of minutes to tell you where your work would fit into the overall picture, why and when it was needed. They might even have asked you whether you understood their instructions, or enquired how you were thinking you'd go about the task they'd given you. Most importantly, they'd have taken responsibility for setting an atmosphere that made it easy for you to seek clarification and to make your best contribution.

Another thing you can squeeze out of your past experience is the knowledge that the world can seem very different to people sitting on opposite sides of the same desk. Everything might make sense to you, with your complete knowledge of the project and its timetable and your role in the decision making. But the junior's mind might be a confusion of pressures and deadlines they don't understand; burdens that you could lift straightaway if only you remembered for a moment what it was like to do their job.

The tolerable gap

You might be frustrated because you have people you're meant to delegate to but you know you could do the task better yourself.

Stop for a second. Did you really fall into such an obvious trap? Surely, it would be a sad state of affairs if you couldn't improve on a piece of work produced by someone who reports to you?

What lies behind that difference in output? It could be down to training or experience. In either of those cases, things are only going to improve with further opportunities and by people like you doing your job as a mentor. Before you blame anyone else, look in the mirror and consider what you can do to make things better.

What aspects of your junior colleague's work do you pick on to correct? Can you (and do you) explain what they've got wrong and what they need to do differently next time? Are you changing things because they're incorrect, or because they're not in the style that you'd use yourself?

When you challenge yourself, you might see aspects of your colleague's work that do the job perfectly adequately, even though they don't reach your own dizzy height of perfection or quite exhibit your style. I suggest that you persuade yourself to tolerate the efforts that fall into that gap. Let go, and see the positive effect on your colleague's confidence and engagement.

You have a choice. You can either encourage your colleagues to work in their own style, or you can insist on every piece of work looking exactly as though you had produced it yourself. If you take the second route, you're missing the point of delegation; you're committing yourself to unnecessary hours of dull and frustrating endeavour, you're placing a limit on what your team can produce and you're denying your colleagues the chance to flourish and to outgrow you.

Even when you've got time

Usually, we're promoted because we've been diligent over a period of time, not because we've sat back and come up with useful ideas. Hard work and attention to detail have been so much at the centre of our work that we can tend to dive back into the comfort they offer, if we're given half a chance.

It can be hard to delegate when you know you'd do the job more quickly yourself. But be honest and face up to the truth that you're making a choice. It's for you to gauge whether that choice is the right one, but for the sake of speed, and maybe to make you feel more comfortable about your own contribution, you're stealing from your colleague their opportunity to gain experience.

Is speed of delivery really so important on this occasion? Or would nothing be lost by using this task for a model exercise in delegation, with your colleague learning more about their job and you gaining vital experience of delegating?

Don't say 'just'

Show respect for the time and good efforts of your colleagues. Many fine words and actions can be thrown away in an instant, without that being your intention. Make it a rule for yourself never to use the word 'just' when you're delegating. 'Can you just…' makes whatever the task would be sound by-the-way and worthless.

Delegate: practical steps

1. Apart from the task, think about the team, what it produces and what shape it's in
2. Be clear – What needs to be done, by when?
3. Check that they've understood; keep open a channel of communication
4. Encourage efficiency, not fear (if the team fails, you've failed)
5. Delegate even when you could do it better
6. …even when you could do it more quickly
7. Don't say 'just'
8. Let go!

3.9: Manage Your Manager

If you boast to your friends and family that your firm has a clear strategy, that you work in a supportive, well organised structure; always know exactly what's expected of you, that you are respected, and receive encouragement and praise just when they're due, then you're probably unique. It's infinitely more likely that you have a few things you grumble about.

As human beings, we like to focus the blame on someone else. It's more helpful if it's just one person: the longer we make the list, the more we risk concluding that it can't be that everyone else is wrong, and that maybe we might bear some of the blame ourselves. And it can't be the people who report to us who are at fault. That one quickly rebounds to whoever takes responsibility for them, and we know what that means. So it's the firm and our boss who are lacking.

You're making a choice

In this situation, you have three options.

Before you go any further with this, be honest with yourself and accept that, whichever route you take, you're making a choice.

You're making a choice even if you decide on Option One, which is 'Do Nothing, carry on as before'. In some situations,

'Carry on as before' works magnificently well. And it's up to you. Just bear in mind that, when you make the choice, you're then responsible for what that choice brings. Don't be surprised, though, if doing the same as before brings exactly the same results as it did in the past.

Option Two is the Nuclear Option. Leave. People do leave firms. They even leave particular bosses.

Or there's Option Three, which might merit serious consideration. Be your own boss.

Step back from your situation and accept that it might be a bit weak of someone with your skills and ability to be waiting for someone else to tell them what to do. You might be selling yourself short.

It doesn't really matter why clearer guidance isn't reaching you; perhaps there simply isn't a plan to tell you about; perhaps your boss isn't bursting with ideas or doesn't set the world on fire when it comes to communication. Whatever the reason, maybe you owe it to yourself to push yourself more, not simply to wait, especially if the only prize you get for waiting is a solid excuse for keeping on grumbling.

If there's blaming to be done, how about blaming yourself for failing to take the controls when you can? If your boss doesn't treat you with respect, doesn't let you know what's going on or encourage your ideas, and if you find that treatment demeaning, I suggest you recognise that you're on the spot to choose one of the three Options. You can choose to go along with things, or find another job, or you can make a start on doing what you think your boss is failing to do. You can treat yourself with respect. If you act downtrodden, you'll be downtrodden. Respect your own time, for example, in the way that you feel a good boss would respect your time.

That means giving yourself a break when a fair boss would do, but it also means getting on with things when your idea of a fair boss would expect you to do so.

If the brief isn't completely clear, you can (gently) submit your view and, while you're about it, practise your own clear communication skills. That better way of doing things might even catch on.

And if it's praise you're missing, you do have to remember that (in most cases) you're not working for the Salvation Army. If you need it, though, I suggest you find your own way of marking when you think you deserve a pat on the back.

Don't sit there waiting to be spoon-fed by your boss, you owe it to yourself to do more than that. In fact you don't just owe it to yourself...

While your boss is blind to their shortcomings, what about the log in your own eye? When you gripe to your colleagues about your latest frustration, how long will it be before they're agreeing amongst themselves that you're just the same yourself? Do you show respect for the people who work around you, keep them informed and welcome their ideas? Does each of them feel appreciated by you?

If you're frustrated by what you see as your firm's or your boss's failure to do what you'd do if you were in charge, I suggest that you make for yourself a list of those shortcomings. Then challenge yourself with the question 'What can *I* do about that?' You might not be in a position to change the whole firm, but perhaps you could make a difference in a smaller part of the organisation. And, after you've looked upwards, have a careful look down to make sure you've not become a critic who fails to look after their own team.

There's a neat and happy conclusion to this line of thinking.

When bosses are asked what makes individual employees stand out from the crowd, they never seem to say it's an ability to follow instructions to the letter. They use that word 'proactive', and they describe that special person as the 'self-starter', who doesn't wait to be told exactly what to do, but comes up with ideas and gets to work on them without prompting.

The price of inertia

In case you're still thinking the 'Do nothing' option is the one to choose, think again.

Are you content to let this particular boss dictate the limit of your career? The mere fact that they're your boss doesn't mean they're more talented than you are. Maybe they just got there first. And as you gather your thoughts on things that you can see and that your boss is missing, perhaps you're stacking up the evidence that shows why you really should go on to greater things than they've achieved.

Wouldn't you be letting yourself down if you allowed someone like that to hold you back? Don't you owe it to your future self to get active and find a way to do the managing yourself?

Manage your manager: practical steps

1. Ask yourself:
   - *What's missing – what is it my boss isn't doing? What difference does it make?*

- *Does it matter?*
2. Challenge yourself:
- *What can I do to fill this gap?*
3. Tell yourself:
- *Whether I do something or whether I do nothing, I'm making a choice.*

3.10: Balance Work and Life

Before you blame anyone else, consider what limits you think would be right for someone like you doing your kind of job. How many hours or days at a stretch? How many (if any) consecutive weekends devoted to work? Should you ever switch off your phone for work communications? And if you should; when? And for how long?

Next, you'll have choices to make and communicating to do.

If you choose to limit your working time from 9.30 am to 5.30 pm each weekday, with an hour off for lunch, you're very clearly selecting a way to protect yourself from the strains that a busy career might bring. At the same time, though, you'll have to be realistic about whether that level of engagement will fit the kind of career you want to develop. Those hours might work well for some careers, but don't expect anyone to take you seriously as the person to go to when they're in urgent need of legal advice, for example.

When you think about 'work/ life balance', don't think of everything that counts as 'work' as bad.

The phrase 'work/ life balance' wasn't in use until the 1970s. It wasn't a rallying call for the downtrodden masses Dickens and Orwell wrote about. And it wasn't brought in to plead the cause of the last remaining coal miners; it was a weapon that was deployed, not on behalf of manual labourers, but for a privileged category of people who had chosen careers that ended up hijacking their lives.

It's time we recognised this phrase was out of date before it was coined. And a bit of honesty will shine a more constructive light on this subject. We talk about our offices as the 'coalface'. But a real coalminer would not have been amused. Our offices are well lit. In winter, they're warm; and we've even got used to them being cool in summer. Those auditors who inhabit dimly lit basements are the exception that proves the rule. Working from home, many of us have even more influence over our surroundings.

What do we spend our time at work actually doing; and is it all so bad? Again, I suggest we're fortunate. We aren't repeating conveyor-belt tasks through a mind-numb 'shift'. In the commercial world, we're interacting with colleagues and clients, we're solving problems and we're communicating. What aspects of your job do you admit you enjoy? You might even allow yourself a smile: maybe the person who chose that career for you didn't go so far wrong after all?

We start to see a bit of blurring between 'work' (what we get paid for) and 'life' (the bits we're meant to enjoy). We're not always quick to admit, even to ourselves, that we like some of what we do at our 'coalface'. You might have colleagues who are fathers with very young children (you might even be one yourself) who say they get into the office early when they can, because, that way, they get more done. Too right! Especially when they can leave someone else at home to do all that early morning childcare. I suggest that's a clear example of a choice being made, where 'work' isn't a pit of toil but, instead, it represents the more comfortable option.

Beyond that example, I challenge you to conduct a test at random points in your working day. The plain question to ask yourself is, 'Am I (honestly) enjoying this?' You don't have to share your answers with anyone. In fact it might be a bit strange if you did. Choose your own words to describe how you feel, but what you'll find is that it varies. And if you're honest, you'll accept that parts of your job are actually how you'd choose to spend your time even if you had a choice...which, of course, you do!

Recognising the good bits helps us to see we're not just labouring away under a dark cloud of 'work'. The chances are there are strands of light and shade in our work time, not so very different from that 'life' time for which we're not getting paid. If we really can't come up with anything good about our job, we can either focus on who's to blame (but what's the point of beating ourselves up?), or we can take responsibility for making our role more fulfilling, or for finding a different role that is.

Instead of pointing an accusing finger at that evil 'work', we might step back, better to see the bigger picture, and take responsibility for aligning how we spend the whole of our time (whether paid or not) with our values and with what interests us.

Be honest with yourself about where your boundaries lie. This isn't a simple matter of deciding what hours you'll work and deciding what times you'll start and finish every day. When do you get tired? What makes you stressed? On the other side of things, do you get a positive thrill, a sense of pride, feel needed and recognised when you're called on for help?

As the context and your mood change, your boundaries– the limits of what you want to put up with – will change too.

Having done your thinking, now you'll have to communicate. Don't waste your time and energy resenting colleagues who seem not to notice or care that there's too much toil in your day. Only you know where your boundaries are now and how they're likely to change. The challenge for you is to work out what to say, how and when to say it, and who to say it to.

Balance work and life: practical steps

1. Notice when you're enjoying 'work'
2. Be honest and admit (to yourself, at least!) when your job's actually all right.
3. If your work/ life balance is under threat, ask yourself: Who's doing the threatening – is it someone else, or is it me? Where are my boundaries?
4. Who do I need to tell?
5. When should I tell them, and what words should I use?

3.11: Manage Stress

This is not aimed at anyone who is affected by stress at the level of a medical condition.

Most of us get a rush out of working to a deadline; we can be carried along by the momentum of operating in a hurry, and we can feel a sense of achievement when we've got things done in time. And it's not just about deadlines. We like the idea that we've reached or exceeded exacting standards.

Let's not call everything we do in a hurry 'stressful', as if we resent it. And let's not paint ourselves as victims every time we're set a task that requires us to achieve a high standard.

The most helpful commentary I've read on stress likens it to bending a piece of metal or stretching a piece of elastic. To an extent, that bending or stretching is fine, but not if it's too severe or if it goes on too long.

It's important that we try to understand ourselves and the people around us. What kind of metal are we; and what state of health/mind/mood are we in just now for bending and coming back into shape? We need to be alert to when there's some bending or stretching going on, or, better still, we need to develop a sense of when that test is coming around the corner.

And then we need to decide what we're going to do about it.

Who creates your stress?

My experience tells me there are three culprits pretty close to home.

The obvious one is the boss, or the company, or the system. That's the slave-driver above you. You can't do anything about it because they're in charge and that's just the way it is.

I challenge you to question that conclusion. It's easy and lazy to accept the status quo. If you see your relationship with your manager as a one-way street, you've signed up to subservience. Maybe your boss isn't on a deliberate evil mission to make your life hell. Maybe they just don't know what stress they're creating; and maybe they lack the skills or experience to know what to do in this situation. Perhaps you can say some carefully chosen words to help. One thing's for sure, telling everyone else you know, apart from your boss, about what stress your boss brings to your life isn't the shortest route to improving things.

We're quick to identify other people who make our lives difficult. But what about looking in the mirror for culprit number two? Who makes you sit at your screens for quite so many hours in the week? And who's really responsible for accepting all the tight deadlines? Is it always down to someone else, or, if you're honest, are you the one who so often tightens the screw? The chances are you're not in a role where meek subservience is the only possible way. Much of the time, you're making a choice. But, being human, you'll want to reserve the right to complain about the choice you've made.

My suggestion here is that you open your eyes. Recognise that you're very often the one who volunteers those short deadlines. You have a choice: you can be more realistic, brave and honest (with yourself and with others) about what you can achieve; or, alternatively, you can accept that you know exactly who you should blame for the tense situation you've dumped yourself in.

I'm not saying it's always your fault. But look out for the choices you have to make and be aware of what you'll be bringing upon yourself by volunteering that too-short deadline.

Culprit number three is you as the manager. You set the tone. As lawyers would say, it's strict liability. No excuses: if the people working for you are stressed, it's your fault.

You're not actually evil, or on a mission to make anyone's life unliveable, so how have you allowed stress to build up around you? Maybe you think stress is par for the course (you're wrong, it's not). Maybe you think the happiness of the people who work for you is no part of your job (you're wrong, it is). Maybe you lack skills or training (be honest with yourself); or maybe you simply hadn't picked up that there was a problem?

You might have noticed a connection between culprits one and three. The managed and the manager can do each other and themselves a favour with a bit of honest communication.

Think, be brave, and communicate

When we know we have to get something done with some level of urgency, that can help us to keep moving and to operate efficiently. There's a difference, though, between a healthy degree of pressure and what we would recognise as

73

'stress'. Stress can bring 'red mist', that mind-blocking state when your head feels filled with cotton wool, your brain is flooded, the simplest decisions seem like mountains to climb, and you're left exhausted. Looking back on a period of stress, you can see that your 'bandwidth' for thinking was constricted and reduced, meaning your mental resources were lessened at exactly the time when you needed them most.

If only you could manage things so that you could fend off the red mist and have all your thinking power available when it's most called for.

Timing your intervention is all-important. Once you're actually under stress, you'll find it difficult to detach, make an objective assessment of your situation and work out a solution. Get used to looking ahead. What's that coming over the hill...? Is it something that's likely to bring you stress? What is going to cause that stress, and what can you do about it?

At this early stage, while you have the luxury of being able to think clearly and objectively, press yourself to identify where the difficulties are likely to arise. Do you understand what's expected of you? Do you have all the facts you need to do what you have to do? Do you have the resources, skills, training and experience that are called for? Is the deadline realistic?

If you fail to address these likely obstacles, you're storing-up your own secret burden – a sure route to stress. Be fair to yourself and find the right words to tell your boss or your client what will need to change.

Those deadlines

Is that really the deadline? What's likely to happen if the deadline's missed?

If, working diligently and imaginatively, you won't be able to meet that deadline, you'll either need more resource or you'll need to change the deadline.

Stop, and sharpen the saw

In his 1989 book '*The 7 Habits of Highly Effective People*' Stephen R Covey made a suggestion for what we'd say if we were watching a lumberjack chopping down trees. As the man becomes exhausted by his efforts and his saw loses its cutting edge, the logic of Covey's suggestion is crystal clear. We wouldn't be urging the lumberjack on to more physical effort. Instead, we'd see the greater value in him stopping, taking a break and sharpening the saw.

Be the one to make that suggestion, for yourself and for others, next time you see 'stress' coming over the horizon.

Manage stress: practical steps

1. Think, and talk to your colleagues about stress when things are calm
2. Ask yourself:
  - *When have I felt stress?*
  - *What made me feel stress?*
  - *In the same situation now, what could I do to make things better? What makes my colleagues feel stress?*
6. Make sure deadlines are explained and justified
7. Stop, and sharpen the saw!

3.12: Be Lucky!

It wasn't Napoleon, but someone rather less well known (Cardinal Mazarin, Chief Minister of France, 1642-61) who came up with that statement we thought we knew about lucky generals. It seems that it was Mazarin, who said, 'the question to ask of a general is not: "Is he skilful?", but "Is he lucky?"'

So much for the detail, what about the principle?

Richard Wiseman is a brilliant and fascinating academic– also a stand-up comic and a magician – who carefully researched luck, what distinguishes 'lucky' and 'unlucky' people and what we can all do to improve our luck.

Wiseman and his colleagues built a cohort of several hundred people who defined themselves as either 'lucky' or 'unlucky'. Work then began on assessing whether these groups really were different from each other.

One basic test was to ask what numbers they favoured for the UK's national lottery. Apart from one exception (on which, more below), the results showed that, on average, everyone lost – apart from the lottery organisers – and to the same degree.

People were inconsistent in assessing their 'luck'. One woman with a history of misfortunes described herself as the luckiest person in the world, while a lottery jackpot winner explained that he was unlucky because his success hadn't come on a 'rollover' week.

One exercise that Wiseman devised identified the real difference between those who were lucky and those who weren't. He challenged them to put together the pieces of a complex three-dimensional puzzle. One type of person tended to give up early: 'With my luck, I'll never be able to do this!' but others persisted – and with better results. That persistence made the difference between them.

Maybe we should call it 'positive thinking', belief, perseverance, or resilience, not luck.

From his research, Wiseman developed a number of principles, all reflecting the truth that we make our own luck.

Don't blame fate, don't dwell on the negatives, get on with the stuff you *can* change, and take responsibility for your own good fortune!

If you get a chance to see Richard Wiseman speak, grab it! His books (he's written a lot) include *The Luck Factor* (Random House, 2003), *Did you spot the gorilla? How to recognise hidden opportunities in your life* (Random House, 2003) and *59 Seconds: Think a Little, Change a Lot* (Pan Macmillan, 2009).

Richard Wiseman told me about another research project he'd run; this one focused on establishing whether ghosts really do exist.

As with his work on luck, he approached the subject with scientific rigour. And again, killjoy that he is, he concluded that there's no such thing: like luck, ghosts are a construct of our imagination.

There's a common thread here: there's no point waiting for the fates to sort out our challenges, we need to wake up to the fact that it's all down to us to take responsibility and take control.

Be lucky: practical steps

1. Give yourself a talking-to: there's no such thing as Luck.
2. Take responsibility.
3. Take control.
4. Get on with the things you *can* change.

Part 4: Tools for Tackling Change

In this section I describe a variety of techniques you can use to tackle the twelve challenges in section 3 or any other challenges that might come your way.

4.1: (Really) Listen, Look, 'Notice'

You're in the street, holding a conversation, and a pneumatic drill starts right next to you. Plainly, you can't hear what's being said to you, and your conversation has to pause until the distraction has stopped.

That's a very clear example of 'noise' that prevents you hearing what's said to you.

I invite you to be on the alert for other 'noise', interference that's much more subtle than a workman's drill. In this context, I mean anything at all that intrudes and prevents you from absorbing the full meaning of what's being communicated to you.

The interference might be something that you can hear, like background music or raised voices, drawing away some of your attention. There might be something you can see out of the corner of your eye, or over the shoulder of the person who's talking, and it's that other thing that's taking over part of your thinking. It might even be that there's a physical distraction that's diverting your attention from what's being said to you.

Even when you've cleared the stage of these intrusions, you might still have more work to do before you can *properly* listen to what's being said to you. Be honest with yourself.

Have you got other thoughts coming into your mind, maybe about what else you've got to do before your next appointment, or what you might buy to cook this evening? You will have to clear your mind of those other thoughts before you can hope to communicate to the other person that you're interested in what they're saying or hope to understand what they really have to say.

Having quelled the 'noise', you're ready to listen.

Listening is sometimes more than just recognising words that are spoken to you. It can be a fascinating detective game.

Imagine you're playing a game that's a bit like Charades, but much more complicated and much more fun. Of course, I'm not including simple transactional conversations here; I'm referring to situations where the person you're listening to holds a secret, about their true thoughts, feelings, or intentions. The exciting twist is that they might not know themselves the real nature of what's on their mind or what they are likely to do about it.

In this game, unlike Charades, within reason, you can ask the person with the secret whatever questions you like, and they can speak to you as freely as they wish. That sounds easy. But what if they haven't really got their thinking sorted out, or what if it suits them not to disclose their real feelings and intentions? This is where the fun comes in. You need, in your mind, to move your chair a little closer, to focus your microscope a little more crisply.

Apart from the words that are being spoken, what does the tone tell you? How about the facial expression? What about the more general body language?

Back to the words, is anything being repeated? Sometimes, people use the same expression more than once without realising what they're doing. When that happens (and so long as you notice it), you're getting a better understanding of their thoughts than they have themselves.

The rules aren't quite as simple as I might have suggested. The truth is, you can listen to what's said to you and watch carefully, but if your 'funnelling' or 'drilling down' (the awful jargon that gets used for those focused follow-up questions) is rumbled and resented your game will come to an abrupt end. You need to remember that your conversation is between people, not machines, and you need to adapt your style of listening to the personality you're dealing with.

If you've got the appetite for reading more about listening, try Nancy Kline, for example *Time to Think, Listening to Ignite the Human Mind* (Cassell Illustrated, 1999).

4.2: Step Back and Look at the Machine

Your attention and energy taken up completely by the task in hand, you're 'getting on with the work', and it's taking a lot out of you.

Surely, that's success, of a kind? Busy must be good? And those long hours that make you feel like you're a martyr to the firm's cause surely place you beyond criticism, whether that's from your colleagues or from you yourself?

You can't stop and reflect on your situation, anyway. You'll leave that sort of thing to colleagues with more time on their hands.

You can do better than this. Stop.

Stand back and look at the machine. Whether that machine is your team, or just you.

What mode are you operating in right now? Is this business as usual (smooth running), are you in crisis (gritting your teeth 'til it's over, patching things up and surviving), or are you creating new ideas (gaining new ground)?

How's the machine looking? Does it need some fine tuning? Is it running too hot? Are any parts coming under stress?

Detach yourself.

What would a spectator on the side-line see?

4.3: Re-Assess

It can take bravery to stop and check if you're heading in the right direction.

If you're bent on some solo task, you might not want to risk the disappointment of finding out your efforts so far have been off target, even though you know you're avoiding the truth. If you're in a group, all the more if you're in charge, you've got extra obstacles in your way. You don't want to slow everyone down, and it would be easier to grit your teeth and hope for the best than entertain the possibility of losing face: what if it turns out that you've been leading your troops in the wrong direction?

Surely, though, if you're in any doubt, better to stop and check, and sooner rather than later? Think of the boost you'll get from confirming you're doing the right thing, or from making a change now, before the situation gets worse.

It's a time to bring yourself into line and, briefly at least, be logical, not 'human'. Daniel Kahneman *(Thinking, Fast and Slow),* and Richard Thaler (*Misbehaving* (Penguin Books, 2016)) write fascinatingly about how we make decisions. Thaler's book explores many ways in which real people differ in their decision making from the fictional 'homo economicus', or 'Econ' (imagine a version of Mr

Spock from Star Trek). Econs provide the purely objective, logical model upon which economic predictions are based. Humans 'misbehave', or take decisions different from those their Mr Spock-cousins would take, often in ways that are not in our best interests.

Having made that brave but logical decision to re-assess, make the most of the exercise and avoid falling into the most obvious of traps that is always waiting for any of us humans to fall into.

Kahneman and Thaler both write about the 'sunk cost fallacy'. Thaler describes a tennis player who keeps on playing despite injury, because he doesn't want to waste the money he's spent on his annual subscription. If only he'd stepped back and re-assessed his situation objectively, Thaler's tennis player would quickly have seen his folly.

4.4: Conduct Your Very Own '360'

You don't need to click on any links or email any surveys to do this. You do, though, have to take a bit of time, and you need to think.

Up. What frustrates you about your boss? And what behaviours do you admire? Step back and weigh your thoughts. When you do this, you're doing more than listing debits and credits for someone else; you're also highlighting for yourself some habits that you think are important. Do you think your colleagues around you might find those same things relevant to their jobs, too?

Perhaps you feel your boss keeps you in the dark, falling down on communication.

Across. Taking that theme of Communication, how do you think your peers would rate **you**? Might they say about you those very same things you say about your manager? Be honest. Be frank. No one's listening to your thoughts but you.

Down. Now take a different vantage point. Put yourself in the position of each person who reports to you. Take them one by one. In your mind's eye, hand to them that very same telescope that you yourself had focused on your boss. What kind of deal does each individual get from you? Put yourself on the spot, and demand facts. What words would be used to describe you as a communicator? Good or bad, what's the evidence?

When you've done this thinking, what are you now going to change to make things better?

You can cover all of this in a quiet fifteen minutes. Or if you don't have a quarter of an hour to spare; just ask yourself one question: 'What must it be like, working for me?'

4.5: Re-Frame / Flip the Coin Over

In history, when a candidate was being considered by the Catholic Church for canonisation, an important role was played by an official whose title, translated from Latin, was *Devil's Advocate*. That person's job was to argue the other side. To investigate, and to put forward any contrary argument that said this person didn't deserve to be made a saint.

You've probably got a close family member or friend who performs this role for you. Whenever you complain about anything, they'll come up with the other side. You say it's so rude someone's always late for calls or meetings, your colleague says 'Well, they might be very busy,' or 'They might have been held up in traffic,' or 'They've got a very difficult job to do.'

Why can't they just agree with you? You weren't really looking for an answer anyway, but what you hear annoys you. It frustrates you that you're being questioned. And it strikes you this happens a lot. Why do they need to find an opposing argument every time? Another thing that bugs you, though, is that they're often right.

Maybe you can choose to find it helpful when your Devil's Advocate speaks up? And maybe you can pause, turn things over in your mind, and advocate for the other side yourself?

You won't always have the luxury of your contrary-colleague on tap to bounce around the competing views, helping you to make an assessment from all sides.

You might think it is weak, even to contemplate what the other side to the argument might be, but you can do it in your own mind if you want. No one else needs to know. You might nudge your thinking onto a better track, or you might come out with your original view stronger. But you'll have had a good look around and tested for yourself the arguments that might be made against you.

4.6: What Would Your Dream Adviser Tell You to Do?

Alive or dead, real or fictional, who's judgement would you respect? What would they tell you to do in this situation?

You don't even have to limit yourself to one phantom adviser; you can wheel out different advisers for different decisions.

I've worked with clients who would call upon Daniel Kahneman, because Kahneman brings a clear, logical and refreshing method to decision-making, or Ray Dalio, on the basis that he's made so much money he can't be wrong.

But the choice is yours, and it's infinite.

A young Italian client selected Andrea Pirlo. The chances are, you won't have heard of Pirlo, but he was a magical 'play-maker' of a footballer who, over a long career for Juventus and Italy brought calm and shape to frenetic battles on the football pitch. My client felt he could call on Pirlo's sense of strategy to help bring quiet and clear thinking to his business decisions.

4.7: What's Your Advice to You?

Imagine it's someone else in your situation, not you. They ask for your advice.

Before you can help, they'll have to break things down, run through the relevant facts and options, and identify the choices to be made. Then it's over to you...

4.8: Take Control, Take Responsibility

You can sit back and observe that the world's being unfair to you. And you might be right. It may be true that all sorts of things are stacked against you ... A boss who doesn't listen ... Assistants who just don't assist.

If you decide to wallow in your plight, be honest with yourself, and accept you're making the choice to do that. And don't be surprised if nothing improves. At best, you can expect validation – more examples will pile up to confirm your victim status.

But you can make a different choice.

You can take over the driving seat, stop blaming anyone else, and get on with what's needed. Maybe it's your job to do that anyway!

Who Moved My Cheese? (Spencer Johnson – Penguin, 1998) is the tiny book you've seen on the Business shelves of every airport bookshop. Johnson's simple message is that the mouse whose supply of cheese has dried up gains nothing from feeling sorry for itself or wondering who to blame. The only thing that matters is to get on and find some new cheese.

4.9: The G-R-O-W Model

The 'GROW' model can provide a structure for tackling challenges of different shapes and sizes. This approach has been championed by the wonderful Anne Scoular (*The Financial Times Guide to Business Coaching* – Pearson, 2011) and is often central to the thinking of Meyler Campbell-trained coaches (I'll declare an interest: I did my coaching training with Meyler Campbell).

First, what's your **Goal**? (See 3.1 above)

Don't grab the first formulation that comes to mind. When you think you know what your Goal is, stop and question yourself. Be prepared to adjust the Goal so that it really does describe what you want to aim for.

If you find setting your Goal difficult, be fair to yourself – this can be hard for anyone.

Second, test your Goal under the harsh light of **Reality**. Ask yourself some direct questions and be prepared to adjust your Goal if it fails the Reality test. For example, you're interested in wine. It would be nice to know much more about it and a way to achieve that would be to study the subject and pass an exam. How about the Master of Wine qualification? That sounds like a Goal. But have you seen what kind of brain you have to have to complete that highly technical course? Is it 'realistic' to think you can do that? Be honest with yourself. If your answer's no, refine your Goal, or set another one.

Step 3 is **Options**. Imagine a market stall. In your mind, set out along the stall all of the options that are theoretically open to you. Sticking with wine, set out in your mind all of the possibilities you might have for following your interest in learning about that subject. You might sort those options into an order, with 'Master of Wine' at one extreme end, reflecting the difficulty and commitment that would involve. Identify other options, discount those that don't appeal, and make a note to follow up where you'll need more information.

Even after Stage 3, don't allow the concrete to set. You've still got Stage 4 to go.

Reflect now on the Goal you've (almost) established and on the method you've (almost) decided to take towards achieving that Goal. How strong is your **Will** (there's the 'W' of 'GROW') to follow that route? To succeed with the Master of Wine course, you need to be highly intelligent and have the kind of brain that can absorb and retain vast amounts of detailed information (so the Reality test might have stopped you there), and you also have to show an astounding level of application and commitment.

If there's the smallest grain of doubt in your mind, that will only grow. Respect the warning (use your inner voice as a friend (see 3.4)). What do you need to change to make that doubt dissolve? Could you reduce other commitments to have more time to devote to your wine course? Is there help you could seek from someone else? Or do you need to make more tweaks to your Goal before you sign off on it?

Ask yourself, *'Am I really willing to do what's needed?'*, and if you're less than 100% convinced by your reply, you've got more work to do on setting a clear Goal.

You'll know you've taken your work on Goal-setting to the right point when you feel you know where you want to get to, the plan for getting there is clear, and you can mentally sign-off on the theory and hand the blueprint over (to yourself!) for action.

4.10: Will It Make the Boat Go Faster?

Ben Hunt-Davis (Ben Hunt-Davis and Harriet Beveridge-*Will it make the Boat go Faster?* Matador, 2011) was an Olympic oarsman, and then an inspirational speaker. Watching him speak a few years ago, I was struck by the way the audience hung on Ben's every word as he described the build-up to his 2000 Sydney Olympic final and then the race itself, even though they surely knew the outcome (Ben had been billed as an Olympic champion).

Ben's enthusiasm and delightful personality helped to hold our attention as he took us into the elite world of a close-knit rowing team where every suggested change to the regime, whether it was a tweak to the training programme or a new idea on diet, was tested by the question *'Will it make the boat go faster?'*. The single filter was agreed on by the team and it was constantly at the core of the team's purpose.

That laser-focus worked for Ben and his fellow oarsmen, bringing them together and keeping their minds and efforts firmly fixed on the single thing that mattered to them. The result was Sydney Gold for Great Britain's rowing eight.

Words of caution, though, about laser-sharp focus. Anyone who worked with banker (no longer Sir) Fred

Goodwin witnessed an object lesson in single-mindedness. No small talk, no niceties. Every ounce of attention poured into getting from where we were to where Fred had decided he wanted to be.

Fred achieved astounding things in massively expanding The Royal Bank of Scotland, before the bank's spectacular collapse. I suggest that Ben and his teammates were streets ahead of Fred Goodwin in the emotional intelligence stakes. Maybe if Fred had been more of a team player, things wouldn't have turned out so badly for him and his bank.

My advice is to use Ben's test but avoid Fred's error.

Sources

Homer, 'Odyssey', Book 2

Daniel Kahneman, 'Thinking, Fast and Slow', Farrar, Strauss and Giroux 2011; Allen Lane 2011; Penguin Books 2012

Myers-Briggs Type Indicator Instrument (MBTI) (https://www.myersbriggs.org)

Daniel Goleman, 'Emotional Intelligence', Bantam Books 1995

Stephen R Covey, 'The 7 Habits of Highly Effective People', Simon & Schuster 1989

David Maister, 'Strategy and the Fat Smoker', Spangle Press 2008

W Timothy Gallwey, 'The Inner Game of Tennis', Pan Books 1986

Steve Peters, 'The Chimp Paradox', Random House 2011

Ray Dalio, 'Principles', Simon & Schuster 2017

Emilio Galli-Zugaro, Clementina Galli-Zugaro, 'The Listening Leader', FT Publishing 2017

Richard Wiseman, 'The Luck Factor', Random House 2003; 'Did you spot the gorilla? How to recognise hidden opportunities in your life, Random House 2004; '59 Seconds: think a Little, Change a Lot, Pan MacMillan 2009

Nancy Kline, 'Time to Think, Listening to Ignite the Human Mind', Cassell Illustrated 1999

Richard Thaler, 'Misbehaving', WW Norton & Company 2015; Allen Lane 2015; Penguin Books 2016

Spencer Johnson, 'Who Moved My Cheese?', Penguin Books 1998

Anne Scoular, 'The Financial Times Guide to Business Coaching', Pearson 2011

Ben Hunt-Davis and Harriet Beveridge, 'Will it make the Boat go Faster?', Matador 2011

CPSIA information can be obtained
at www.ICGtesting.com
Printed in the USA
LVHW021352270721
693809LV00004B/469

9 781398 406742